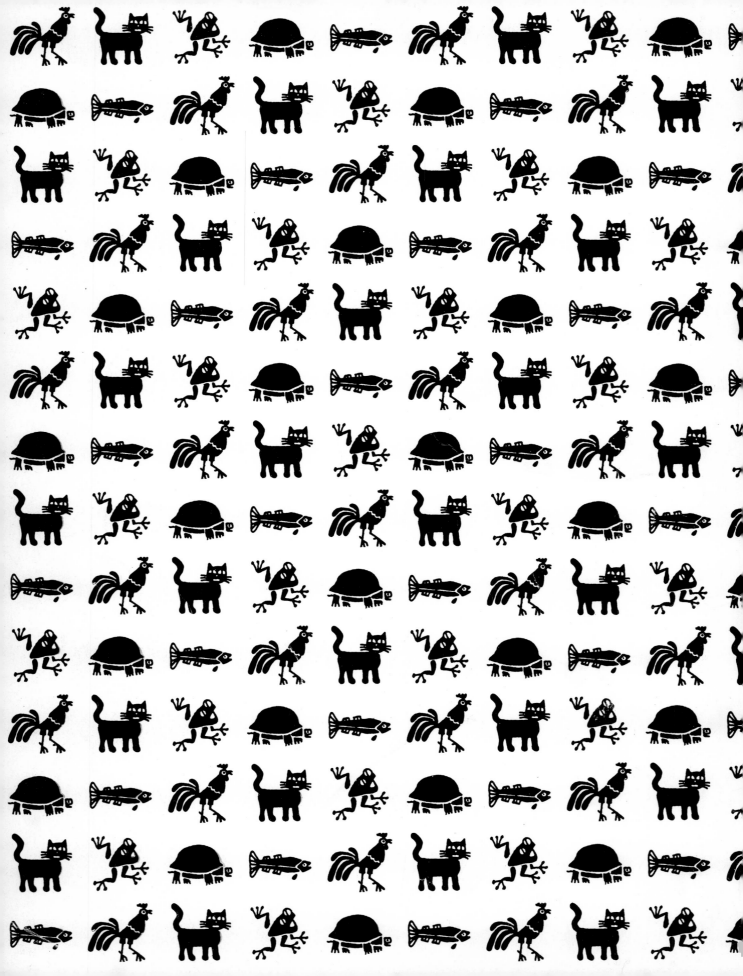

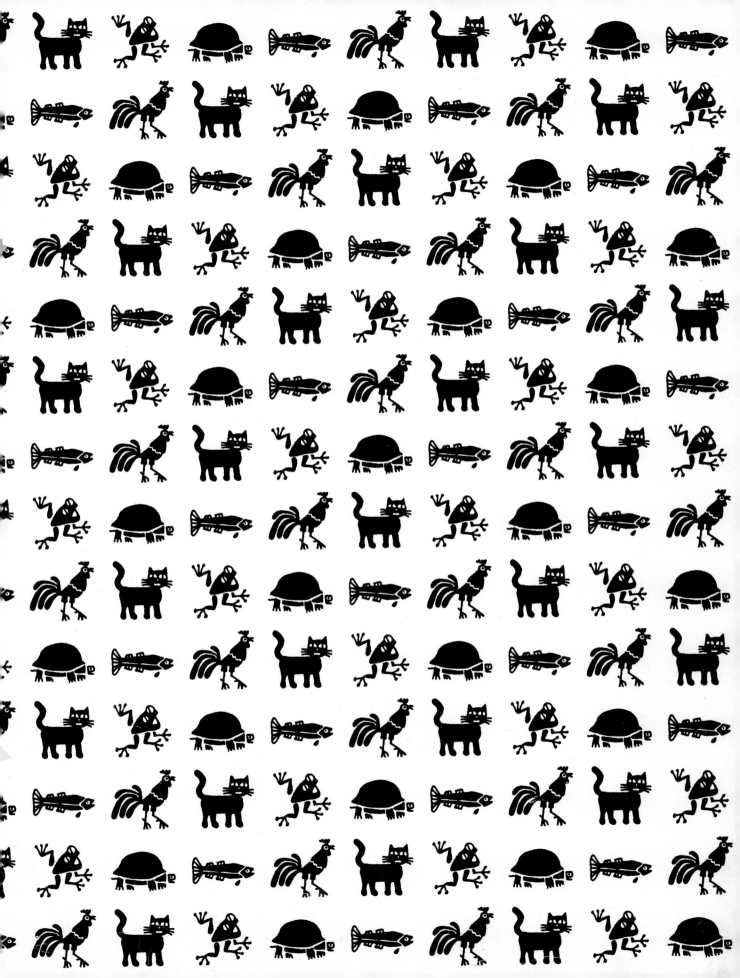

For Benjamin

Franklin Watts, Inc., New York
All rights reserved
Printed in West Germany
L.C.Card 78–171902
SBN 531–02042–8

Eric Carle

The Rooster
Who Set Out to See
the World

Franklin Watts, Inc.
New York, N.Y. 1972

One fine morning, a rooster decided that he wanted
to travel.
    So, right then and there, he set out to see the world.
    He hadn't walked very far when he began to
feel lonely.

Just then, he met two cats. The rooster said
to them, "Come along with me to see the world."
The cats liked the idea of a trip very much.
"We would love to," they purred and set off
down the road with the rooster.

As they wandered on, the rooster and the cats met three frogs. "How would you like to come with us to see the world?" asked the rooster, eager for more company.

"Why not?" answered the frogs. "We are not busy now." So the frogs jumped along behind the rooster and the cats.

After a while, the rooster, the cats, and the frogs saw four turtles crawling slowly down the road. "Hey," said the rooster, "how would you like to see the world?"

"It might be fun," snapped one of the turtles and they joined the others.

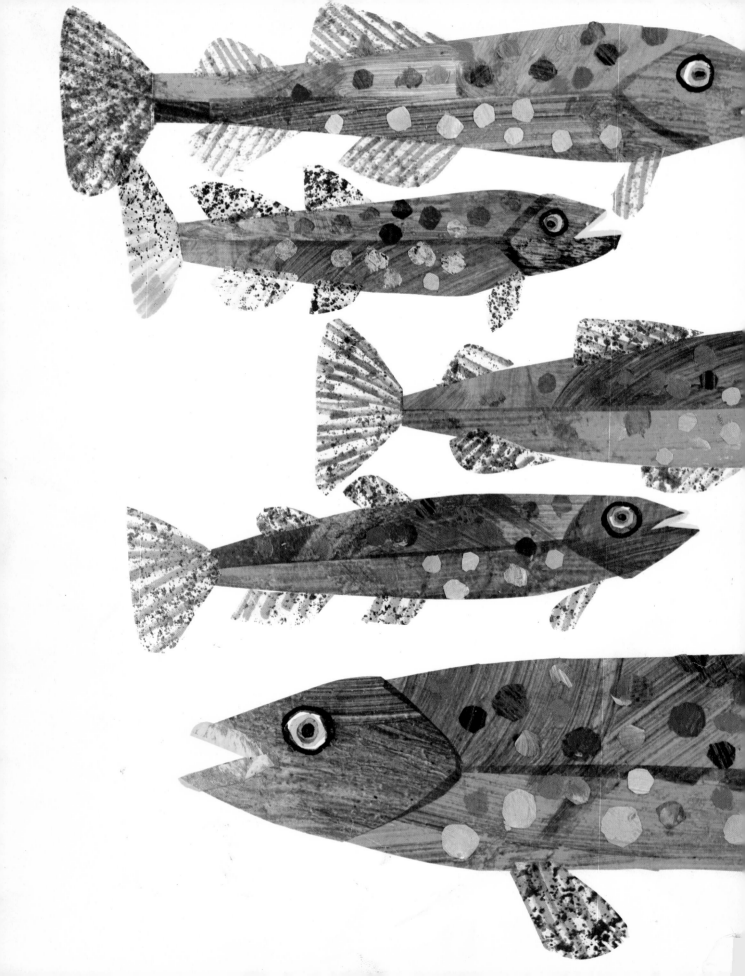

As the rooster, the cats, the frogs, and the turtles walked along, they came to five fish swimming in the brook.

"Where are you going?" asked the fish.

"We're off to see the world," answered the rooster.

"May we come along?" pleaded the fish.

"Delighted to have you," the rooster replied. And so the fish came along to see the world.

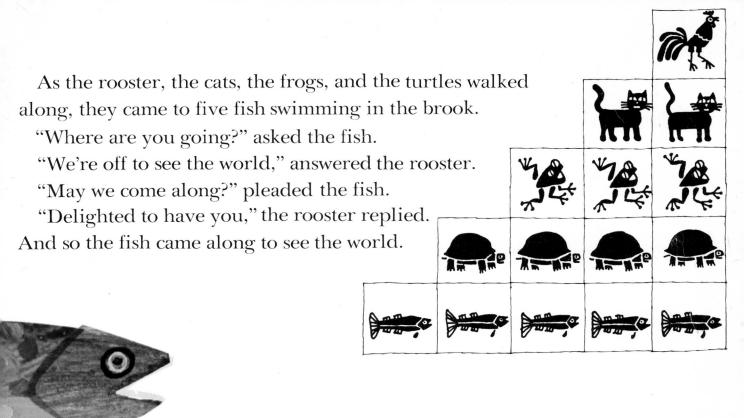

The sun went down. It began to get dark. The moon
came up over the horizon. "Where's our dinner?" asked the cats.
"Where are we supposed to sleep?" asked the frogs.
"We're cold," complained the turtles.

Just then, some fireflies flew overhead. "We're afraid," cried the fish. Now, the rooster really had not made any plans for the trip around the world. He had not remembered to think about food and shelter, so he didn't know how to answer his friends.

After a few minutes of silence, the fish suddenly
decided that it might be best if they headed for home.
They wished the others a happy trip and swam away.

Then, the turtles began to think about their warm house. They turned and crawled back down the road without so much as a good-bye.

The frogs weren't too happy with the trip anymore, either. First one and then the other and finally the last one jumped away. They were polite enough, though, to wish the rooster a good evening as they disappeared into the night.

The cats then remembered an unfinished meal they had left behind. They kindly wished the rooster a happy journey and they, too, headed for home.

Now the rooster was all alone—and he hadn't seen anything of the world. He thought for a minute and then said to the moon, "To tell you the truth, I am not only hungry and cold, but I'm homesick as well." The moon did not answer. It, too, disappeared.

The rooster knew what he had to do. He turned
around and went back home again. He enjoyed a
good meal of grain and then sat on his very own perch.

After a while he went to sleep and had a wonderful
happy dream—all about a trip around the world!

As a child, Eric Carle claims to have been much more of a philosopher than a mathematician. He recalls his difficulties this way:

> If you told me that there were two apples in a bowl and one was taken away and then asked me how many apples were left I wasn't sure. After all, you can't really take away an apple. You can eat it or make cider out of it or hide it under a basket, but the apple is still an apple and it isn't really gone. . . . On the other hand, if you added one apple to a bowl with an apple already in it, there was always the bowl to worry about. Wasn't that a "something" to count in the total?

Eric Carle wrote THE ROOSTER WHO SET OUT TO SEE THE WORLD not only for the child who has these difficulties with numbers as specific symbols, but also for all children who are getting acquainted with numbers. Here visual perception is subtly translated into the specific reasoning involved in contemplating the meaning of numbers and sets.

The author/artist's former inabilities as a mathematician are more than compensated for by his present talents and international reputation as an artist and designer. Born in the United States and brought up in Germany where he studied at the Akademie der bildenden Künste in Stuttgart, Mr. Carle now lives in New York City. His previous picture books include 1, 2, 3 TO THE ZOO, THE VERY HUNGRY CATERPILLAR, PANCAKES, PANCAKES, and DO YOU WANT TO BE MY FRIEND?

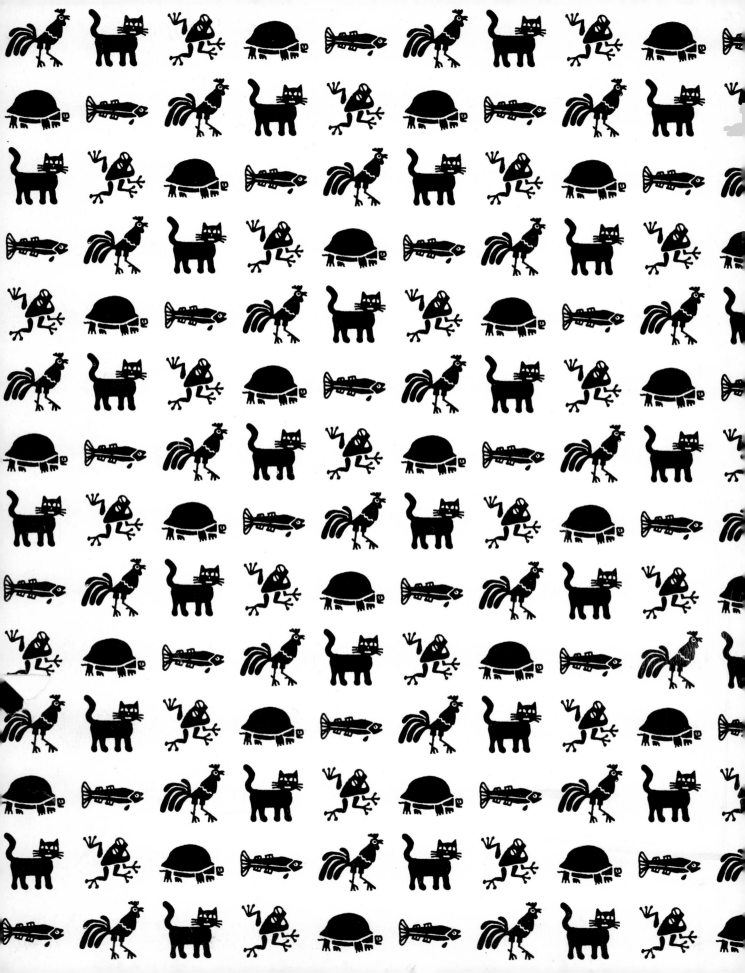

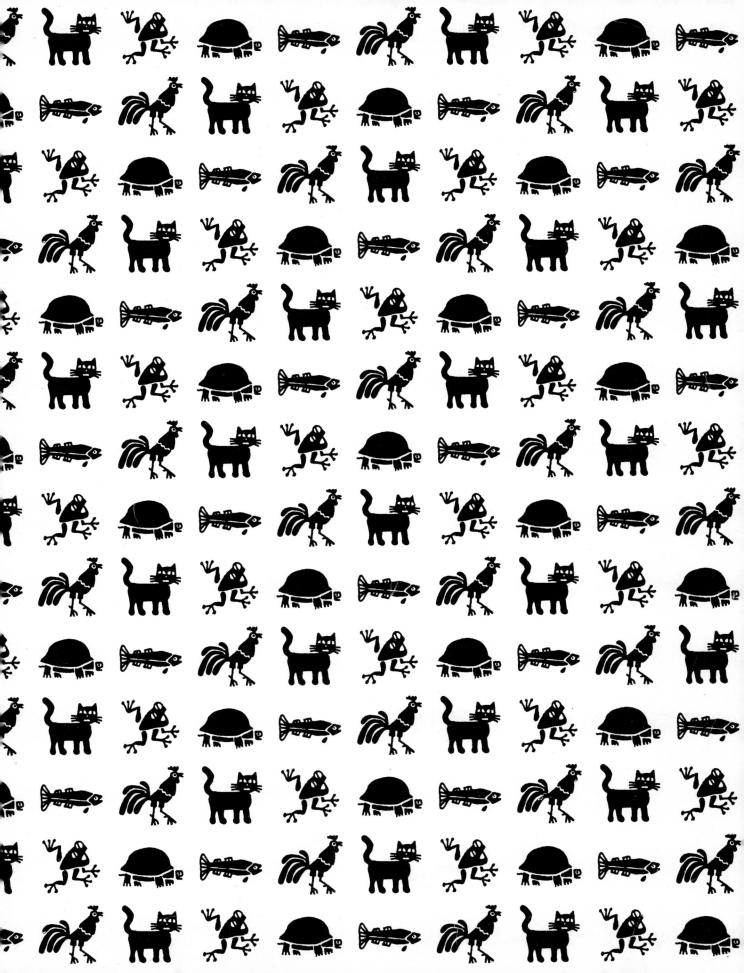